ANOTHER DAY ON EARTH

ANOTHER DAY ON EARTH

Timothy Dekin

TRIQUARTERLY BOOKS
NORTHWESTERN UNIVERSITY PRESS | Evanston, Illinois

TriQuarterly Books
Northwestern University Press
Evanston, Illinois 60208-4210

Printed in the United States of America

10 9 8 7 6 5 4 3 2 1

ISBN 0-8101-5119-7 (cloth)
ISBN 0-8101-5120-0 (paper)

Library of Congress Cataloging-in-Publication Data

Dekin, Timothy.
    Another day on earth / Timothy Dekin.
        p. cm.
    ISBN 0-8101-5119-7 (alk. paper) — ISBN 0-8101-5120-0
(pbk. : alk. paper)
    I. Title.
PS3554.E428 A56 2002
811'.54—dc21

                                        2001006909

The paper used in this publication meets the minimum
requirements of the American National Standard for
Information Sciences—Permanence of Paper for Printed
Library Materials, ANSI Z39.48-1984.

This book is for Elaine.

CONTENTS

ACKNOWLEDGMENTS

The author thanks the editors of the following magazines for earlier publication of poems, sometimes under different titles.

American Scholar: "Community Hospital," "At the Family Plot"
Canto: Review of the Arts: "The Plague"
Poetry Nation Review (Great Britain): "Occasional Uncles"
Sequoia: "White Christmas"
Southern Review: "Flight," "Melancholy," "Letter Home"
Southwest Review: "Elegy at Donner Hot Springs"
Threepenny Review: "The Errand"
TriQuarterly: "The Condolence," "Holly's First Meeting," "Imagine"

"Who Could Ask for Anything More?" was anthologized in *Nine Years After,* edited by R. L. Barth (Florence, Ky., 1989).

"The Plague" and "The Errand" were anthologized in *The Uncommon Touch,* edited by John L'Heureux (Stanford, Calif.: Stanford Alumni Association, 1989).

Many of these poems have appeared in their present or slightly different versions in limited-edition chapbooks over the years: *Occasional Uncles* (Duluth, Minn.: Knife River Press, 1975); *Winter Fruit* (Chicago: Elpenor Books, 1982); *Carnival* (Florence, Ky.: R. L. Barth, 1985); *The Errand* (Florence, Ky.: R. L. Barth, 1989).

ANOTHER DAY ON EARTH

It Used to Be

1

Fear itself changes, the very quality of it—
As, when diagnosed, you "thrill with fear,"
No longer the hypochondriac.

My oxygen machine chuffs and wheezes.
The purple-black seedpods of
Our locust tree litter the walk under my window.

2

It used to be that going fishing
Solved most things short of addiction,
And still I go down to Root River,
My heart not in the killing.

Now, it's the River of No Return for the fall run
Chinook and coho salmon out of Lake Michigan,

And one ill-fated steelhead trout I accidentally hook,
Chrome-bright and fresh:

                              a 12-pound hen I struggle
To release back into the river before its blood
Lactate gets so high it dies anyway.
Silver and purple gill covers jammed open,
It squirts dozens of yellow eggs over my
Hands, waders, cork grip of the rod.
Killing and maiming
Beautiful animals in the wild.
Flyfishing, the quiet sport.

Gasping for breath
That never comes, darkness at the edges
Spreading inward. . . .

Who are You that inhabit so many forms?
Who exists in leaf mold, gill, and splash
Of locust branch
Caught in the stream,
In tiny golden egg-suns dripping upon the stones,
In the hooked, lake-run steelhead gasping for breath?

Who are You
But the cry of anguish and of joy?
(But never my guilt, all mine, all mine.)

Oh end me, too, my unrepentant
And unremitting lashing, my
Slapping at the torrent, at the spray of
Foam, not drinking.

End me, like the black seedpods
Of the locust littering my sidewalk,
The roe caught in the rocks' crevices;
Finish me once and for all, Lord of forms,
Not fighting—
Into your swift flood release me.

The Errand

After so long, I thought the need was gone.
But still I detour by one little bar.
I have re-earned a welcome.
                              I'll buy one
Small glowing cognac to feel up to par,
Which I can drink one handed now, not two,
Or leave it there, radiating near my change,
As it seems most of my new friends can do.
Sipping, I'll take stock. There is stock again
After ten years' saved-up sobriety,
Though mine's a perishable good, I've heard—
Subject to boredom, fear, self-pity, me—
And tallied on a cocktail napkin, blurred
And ringed by the wet impress of my glass,
Adds up to what? A man who won't cause trouble?
Who has a job, friends, credit; whose great task
Is to live normally?
                        Make mine a double.

Here's an oasis where bright waters flash
Chilling reflections of my glistening fur;
Springs leap up from the rocks—I bite at, dash,
And though I keep an eye out on the herd
Slumped in their postures of regret, I meet
My face, amazing in a moon-stunned pool,
And sniff my image till my cheeks are wet
Lifting up from the bar.
                              I scrape my stool.
The noose beside my ear has settled full:
Red loop of neon tubing, my old leash
I almost wish someone would tighten, pull,
That I might find direction, or release;
Some keeper, some orange-emblazoned crossing-guard
To halt the traffic for this wayward dog
Its master has forgotten.

                              No, not today,
I tell myself, today I'll stay outside,
Hurrying along with the homebound crowd
Until I board my usual bus, which stops
For every stoplight, each curb's human freight,
While up above me on a bar of chrome
I see my shiny, miniature face—
Which my hand covers when, as more crowd on,
Swaying a little, I offer up my place.

Aunt Mary

1

Shanty-Irish potato-immigrant from Dublin,
Self-absorbed woman-child
Who yearned for oranges in Watertown's upstate winters,
For lace curtains up on Paddy's Hill;
The second of your sex
                to be put to death
In New York State's electric chair, in Auburn Prison,
Was your sin rabid covetousness?
Did you hate?
Or were you just a poor, feebleminded girl
Who made a bad mistake?

2

"Let the poor woman rest in peace,"
My wife says

When I visit the ancient prison,
My briefcase stuffed full of 1911 newspaper clippings,
In my used SUV,
In my expensive, hand-me-down, father-in-law's suit—
As if to prove the family in complete remission
From poverty, Paddy's Hill, and the bloody trunk.
"A good subject for a novel," I tell her,
Though I mean a good subject
For disconnected rage and guilt—
Aunt Mary, a genetic link from Cain to me?

3

The cell where Mary nursed Peter, her six-month-old,
Ninety years ago is a dayroom now, brightly painted orange;
Gone the execution chamber,
Gone "Old Sparky," the death chair, too.
I can almost smell in the cement walls,
In the alternating bars of steel, the
Chronic, alternating self-love
And self-loathing
                of the underclass.

4

"In the end," the prison chaplain told reporters,
"Mary died a good Catholic."

What did that mean?
That she made a good confession, and was "heartily

Sorry"? That she understood in the flash
Of state voltage that the self always
Counsels grabbing the nearest ax and taking?

Look, she seems to caution me,
Don't hope to distance yourself.
What you call love when you circle your child's
Shoulders to draw his sweetness closer, or your wife's,
Is merely your pleasure,
Wait till they shrug you off,
See who comes first in your own
Heart then.

Beyond the steel-grated windows,
A momentary thunderstorm
Darkens the dayroom like a power surge
Stretching from 1911 to the present.

        5

The day of the murder,
Neighbor Sarah Brennan came down
From the mansion on the hill for the linen
Mary should have laundered by now.
                         Mary's husband
Jim sat in the kitchen drinking homebrew,
The Sobriety Pledge he'd signed still hanging on the wall.
Mary hallucinated that she had two babies,
Or thought that half of the baby
Lay on the rug,

while the other half still nursed.
"Hand me the baby's legs," Mary said to Mrs. Brennan,
"We have to put it back together quickly.
If it lives, I'll be published in the press.
We'll be rich enough to leave this shack."
Jim sat in the kitchen crooning,
"Ah, sweet mystery of life at last I've found you,"
To his homebrew.

Mrs. Brennan complained,
                              "I have a headache.
I'd give you *my* house if you would take
That old ax lying there
                              and knock my brains out."
Or so Mary told the police later.

                6

Out walking for my exercise,
At a crosswalk on the North Shore,
I meet my unmet neighbors:
One of us must give way.
Their black Land Rover starts, and I stare
Them to a stop.
                      Big attorneys downtown
Maybe, or she gets to stay home with the kids
While my wife works and comes home covered
With working.
Their sober Protestant faces seem shocked—
At the furious envy in my own?

7

Aunt Mary, was it for your baby
That you murdered your neighbor
And tried to steal her house?
That when your Peter learned to walk,
He walked as tall
As any Protestant in Watertown?
Culpability isn't the issue here.
The issue is
Original sin.

8

The hand of state electrician Davis
Traces a slow arc behind the curtain.
Only the clicking of the tightening straps
As Mary convulses in the leather harness
Breaks the silence
                  and the murmur of the dynamos—
Mary hovers between two orders of being,
Unable to enter the one
                  without forgiving,
Unable to go back
                  without forgiveness.
Which isn't forthcoming:
A physician applies the death test, noting,
"Some tremors are usual in electrocutions,
Though let's be certain."
Additional current is applied.
Mary forgives and enters the Kingdom of Lucidity.

Our Father, Who art in heaven,
Who fathered Cain,
Who fathered the feebleminded girl-woman
Who made one bad mistake that day
In malignant postpartum depression;
Who fathered the state's all-powerful erection—
Guillotine, gallows, garrote,
Execution chair—
Forgive us our trespasses
As we forgive those who trespass against us.

The Plague

London, 1665

The worst of August. By then, death was no
Item at ale to make us cluck our tongues.
We had run dry of tears. I saw a man
One morning step around a man like dung.

I saw a fisherman place two cod, bread,
And shillings on a rock, then back away
Until his wife retrieved them and walked off.
The rich could leave, but those who couldn't, stayed.

One mother left her children soon enough,
And some said this was evil, some said not:
"Love is a killer," she implored her neighbors,
"It stayed my husband, and now what's he got?"

We were all hoarse from shouting across the street
Or through a door to friends we feared were marked.

The clergy said our plight mimicked our crime;
That we had always guarded heart from heart,

Suspicious, offensive in each other's sight;
That all our charity was only to be liked.
Our Father, and our thieving brother Jack,
Both shunned us, our hearts and pockets left unpicked.

The night the Dog Star set, three thousand felt
Its hot breath and the long rasp of its tongue.
One man chased down his wife and kissed her saying,
"E'en now thou hast it and we'll soon be one."

Despair set in. We knew we were all doomed.
But then the streets filled up: those who had waited
Left hope and fear, ran to the market, church,
The stews, the pubs. And then the plague abated.

Juvenile Hall Teacher

Back from a 12-hour pass,
My student lays her Camel on the desk.
The thin smoke rises in a rope that flutters
A little to her breathing, and her look
Beneath makeup like crayoning is not
The scared look of the cornered animal
I have prepared for, but a knowing smile.

Maria's twelve, a prostitute,
And tortures pets from curiosity.
Trailing her sleeping bag from one abandoned
Building to another,
Like a comic-strip Linus with his blanket,
She's come home forever
To serving lines and dayroom television
And parents with solid black ties.

I yawn, tell her to put the cigarette out
And go and wash her face—

Maria with the tear
A cellmate tattooed on her cheek,
Bleeding before she has begun to bleed.
I offer her the chance to be like me,
Adult, in institutional repose.

Instead, she pulls her blouse up,
Sticks her prepubescent breasts out, her idea
Of a taunt? A sin?
                    I'm touched,
But when she grabs my phone,
I lose it.
            "Give it back!"
I almost shout, You little bitch.
When she shakes her head no
And hides the phone behind her back
I grab the cord coiled round her wrist
And jerk hard.
                    Being on her knees only makes
Her smile more mocking:
We both know what I am
Behind my desk, in my teacher's coat and teacher's tie,
With my pose of weary composure—hell's appropriate behavior—
A synonym for despair.

Calmly as I can, I reach
My hand out for the county's property,
While Maria, raking my forearm with her nails,
Gives me one more chance
To be myself.

Who Could Ask for Anything More?

Simple, he should live in a simpler age:
The elevator man in some hotel;
His limits of responsibility
The gate, clean ashtray stand, clean lift;
His hand upon the lever captain-steady,
His two emotions steady in the crush,
Touch of the cap and a muted, "Going down,"
But soon, in solemn triumph, "Going up!"

Our Lady of Soledad

Circled by candles, lady of sympathy,
With outstretched hands, all robed in blue,
Did my prayers make you pity me,
Or was it your mercy that I turned to you
At all, your love transformed to need in me?—
As, when a mother's milk begins to seep,
The child will wake soon, hungry from its sleep.

Twenty years later I run into her
While touring a mission, surprised that one
So young, so girlish, could have been my mother.
She never has grown up, as I have done,
And when I see her, she seems more my daughter,
Her role reversed, needing my favors now,
My silence about all she shouldn't know.

I leave the mission, taking the old road
Past cyclone fences and the prison
Named after her, translated Solitude,

Where men reside who needed no permission
And asked few favors, hating servitude,
While the women they hurt wait in a row
To visit them, because they're needed now.

Holly's First Meeting

Sometimes her suffering seems beautiful.
That old black magic has her in its spell

Until its wand is broken by her hands
Trembling a silver lighter, or the glands

She counters at the faint, perfumed pulse-place
Behind her ear, but shares with the disgraced.

For her, in Chanel perfume, the correct shoes,
Some church has lent the basement it can't use—

Tables with pamphlets, clean cement decor,
The couches, lamps, and people, pure thrift-store.

She hopes the couches have been sterilized.
She is afraid she will be recognized,

But terrified of blending in. God knows
The shattered alcoholics propped in rows

Deserve one's pity.
                          One man stands and jokes
Away the guilt the last rites couldn't coax;

He wears the world like a loose garment—just
Her size, but she's not buying, not on trust.

She won't fall backward into someone's arms
Except in the most elegant of bars.

Was it her parents who made her this way?
She hated being beautiful when they

Talked about her as if she were not there,
But when they changed the subject, what despair

She left, to show them, on her untouched plate,
Which now she eats for breakfast, cold as hate.

Her doctor/lover still lectures when they meet.
She hasn't changed the cat-box dirt for weeks,

Just put on more perfume, and it's too much.
The cat has bolted.
                          Yesterday at lunch,

Her doctor said he couldn't remain her lover;
He says now that her problem was her father,

Which their affair brought out. She searched her purse
For his new cuff links, gave until it hurt,

Till there was nothing left but these bare walls.
                                        She's
Holly, who always tries so hard to please,

To live up to the perfect self she sought,
Or else get even with herself for not,

Sometimes in church, sometimes beneath a table,
On the floor, in the dirt, among the rabble

Who listen now as she stands up, undressed,
And tells the story no one has ever guessed;

Of old black magic that they know so well,
So laughable, almost too dark to tell.

Imagine

He loved her, but he used his love like rope:
Half hitch, slipknot, thief, figure eight, or noose.
Meanwhile, she found a lover who made love
Seem simple, trite, old-fashioned as a rose.

Now see him smash the pictures that she left,
Then glue them back together in his mind—
That cell where he is always in control
To solve, resist, inflict, and yet be kind;

Or torture himself with pictures of their touch,
Or with a frightening hatred, freeze them to
Statues on an imperishable bed
He must dishevel, strip, change, make anew,

As if those lovers never tired of lust,
Or held each other with a love
That he, too passionate for ordinary feeling,
Cannot imagine being jealous of.

Occasional Uncles:
A Sequence

1. Journal Entry: May 1

So warm we opened up the house today.
The lilacs had come out. I named and took
Lupine and ferns, a blue flower with a white
Eye in its pit—*Brunnera* in the book.

We worked together. Face-to-face, we washed
The cabin windows, rubbing contrariwise.
Cutting through weather, grease, we made almost
Invisible the glass between our lives.

The woods grew quiet and the sun slowed down.
Silent and thoughtless, with nothing to resist,
We were healing and didn't try to talk.
I saw, heavy with light upon my wrist,

Each hair swing slowly with my polishing.
Then drawn by forces I cannot describe,
Lifted from being over redwood plains,
Through burning glass, I entered your clear eyes.

That evening when the neighbor's child came over,
She did not mention as she usually will
The dark character she fears inside the shower,
That lives down in the drain, and causes ill.

2. Do We Belong Together?

Do we belong together, or is there
Some easier love, my synonym, soulmate;
Some image of myself who waits someplace
Unasking, not initiated yet?
Or is it easier to love only me?

I suffer your identity, your needs,
The sacrifice of love—but not for love,
Not for convenience, but because I know
The hypochondriac's old self-concern,
His vigilance, fearing even his sleep
Where he must lose himself, all that there is.

3. It Is

It is
The secrets
Of other women.

It is the sound
Of a night train growing faint
Beyond our room.

It is being
Between points always,
Or out of breath arriving.

It is 4 A.M.
And you have hidden the car keys
For my own good.

4. Flight

The late night flattened to a roar;
Headlong, black road and landscape flood,
As to destruction, to the hood.
Momentum crowds itself for more.

Hurtling defiance, unleashed will!
A motion closing all retreat;
Pure feeling summoned from defeat,
My true asylum, faithful still,

And unironic, chaste as spite.
And when the road blurs, sways with shapes
Where dark, exhausted thought escapes,
Still I bear downward. I was right.

5. Melancholy

Morning, old promise of relief,
Asserts its presence with a light
Unsympathetic, and too bright,
And you are easier with grief,

The amber glowing through drawn shades.
You sit and smoke. Through muted fire
The dust shifts only to expire
On quilt or rug. The bed's unmade,

There's nothing to be gained, or known,
Or saved. Tomorrow you'll be stronger.
Rest here in peace a little longer.
Some cannot make it on their own.

6. Fragment

Streetlights already on at four,
The garbage spilled by dogs, and rain.
And too soon after the last one
I have a hangover again.
I suffer from my memory.
We never learn. Expecting to,
We spoil what we do anyway.
I feel my life start downhill here;
I feel like going to a movie
Convincing as my life, as long,
And in the anonymous dark,
A witness, being entertained.

7. Letter Home

My Dear: Loneliness perfects you here,
Makes strange again what I thought merely mine,
Though if I came back I know you would know
How long that lasts.
                               I just write to say:
This morning with my coffee, with my page
On the bright kitchen table, with secrets near,
Retreat and loneliness I love, I felt
Absence fall like a shadow in the room,
Like one who, drowsing in the afternoon,
Wakens to darkness, and the sense of loss.

8. Her Answer

It's late: your son is struggling in his dream.
The passing cars illuminate the walls
An instant, then the darkness settles back.
I shouldn't write now, not when it's so late,
I should know better and outwait these moods,
As you said often, though you lived by yours.

You couldn't stay home three nights in a row:
I'd hear the beams wince softly as you paced,
Your study closing in, the pages dead,
With nothing to look forward to but me,
And my undressing, familiar as your own;
We two together in one time and place,
Each other's limit and antagonist.

I think about you. I don't know what's best.
I need a husband, not another child.
Some other man may come to warm me here,
To warm his hands, to keep the child and me,
Then your son, with your looks, will be like him,
And our old life will be a passing thought.
If you come home now, keep remembering.

9. Occasional Uncles

The house being strange, my son Sam sleeps with me.
Attentive to his slightest moan or fuss,
I move in answer my disturbing weight
Or cover him, relearning tenderness.

Propped on one elbow, I watch him for hours.
I slowly pull his fingers from his mouth,
Teasing him in his sleep, or hold his two
Feet in my hand, liking the boy too much

When his tense fingers tangle in my beard
To keep me where he's dreaming. I annoy
His sleeping with my kiss. I understand
Those sad, occasional uncles, how they spoil.

10. Sunday, Visiting Day

Your room's no different, but some toys are new.
We kiss. I wonder who gave them to you,
But don't ask. You are almost talking now,
Something I can't quite get about a cow,
A secret conversation you and she
Share, laughing, while I eavesdrop bitterly.
I hug you, gorging myself on the taste,
Touch, smell of you who shrug me off in haste
To play again: you've seen the bright red car
Your friend is holding, playing in the yard.
Your clear face breaking into tears, you run
Shouting, *Mine, mine, mine!* Like father, like son.

Opening Day

Cheyenne, Wyoming

The Medicine Bow Mountains quiver.
The last patches of snow
Are giving up in the shaded places
Like the pale bodies in the hospice,
Slowly as lichen grow,
While in the North Platte River
Cutthroat trout
Like underwater leopards angle upstream
Against the current
As some men hold
Against the dark flow of change.

Spiders, tiny black Romans,
Have engineered the woods
With thousands of taut bright lines
Covering acres
Like a huge stringed instrument.

Breeze strikes a pitch
On the ragged floss,
A soundless vibration
That topples a dead tree
With a scattering of squirrels.

Today is opening day
But you hold stubbornly to the past,
Receding into yourself like the last patches of ice,
Fearing hooks everywhere
And calling it living—
Today is opening day
And the horizon's
Filled with a pink and orange light,
Same color as a wild trout's belly.

Lt. Colonel Dekin,
Squadron Commander,
1944

Over seventy bullet holes from small-arms fire
(They were that low in the windmilled Dutch sky)
Froze the 82nd troopers, squatting on their "steelpots"
In the hold of his squadron-leading C-46 transport aircraft.
Monty's Market Garden operation was a colossal snafu.

"I almost shit my pants," Dad admitted that night
At the Officers Club in Brenthaven, England.
Converting to Catholicism, he flew the second day
Of the mission anyway, winning the Distinguished Flying Cross
To pin beside his Croix de Guerre from D day.
He was twenty-nine years old
And more handsome than the actor Van Johnson, my aunt said.

When he came back to Ilion, New York,
They had to pry me from my mother's neck

When he reached out to hold me for the first time.
I wanted no part of him.

Except at my insistence,
He seldom talked about the war.
Those who had been in it didn't,
He hinted.

Which made it all the more wonderful.
Two Wehrmacht helmets hung from nails
In our garage and Maury Goldman, encyclopedia salesman
By night and police chief by day, nailed me and Bud Fitzgibbons
For impersonating officers when we wore Dad's Ike jackets
With the silver eagles still sewn on.

"I thought you'd want to know," the chief said, winking
Conspiratorially. Laughter and a Ronson lighter appeared
Before Dad could shake a Camel from his pack.

Those were the years of my judging him,
Of my lies that came as easily as breath,
Of angry and unfinishable meals,
Of the seven-state All-Points Bulletin
When I ran away a thousand miles.
It was as if, fleeing home,
I had finally risen
From my bucket seat in the C-46,
Groped my way to the jump door, and
"Hit the silk."

Today, with my own toddler son at the park,
I catch my breath

On a green snail mounted on a coiled spring,
And watch the sky for blossoming ack-ack fire.

Instead, the last of the November sun
Lights up the tops of trees, their bare branches
A rich brown against a pale blue sky.
I flash on something I hadn't thought
Of for forty years: a favorite marble, an aggie,
Swirly brown and blue, so rare!
At the time,
It meant a hundred times more to me than my father did.

When my brother told me, "After Dad was diagnosed,
He cried in the examination room,"
I saw him in a different light.
Too late by then.

Maybe they all were hard-shelled, those men
Who grew up in the depression, cheap with a dime,
Cheap with their affection, cheap with their time;
Maybe a lot of guys, home from the war,
Greeted their children, already three and four,
For the first time,
Too late by then.

At the end, religious junk,
Luridly painted devotional cards of Jesus, Mary,
And the Saints littered his crank-up bed.

His last words to me,
When I had rushed to his bedside but had forgotten
To buy the lottery card he'd

Paid me for, were
"You asshole!"
He was in great pain at the time . . .
"Oh, Timmy, you asshole," he said.
Though I believe he loved me all the same.

White Christmas

1

Holiday Inn, white musical he loves,
Is gusting with "Let It Snow." Then the pain moves

And trips the dancers at their highest kick.
Eleven minutes from codeine. He'll click

Through channels to "A Millionaire," and pray
For snow to cover up the house till May.

Guessing by last night's groans how long he'll last,
His wife feels guilty. Crying breaks a fast.

Who will be left to know her as he knows?
No more or less than children would suppose,

She stirs the gravy, then goes on a spree
Of rich self-pity, like adultery,

And she deserts him.
                        He can hear the noise
Of fighting from the disappointed boys.

Downstairs, the newly sober son forgets
Everything but the bright-as-vodka net

Of tinsel he hangs on the tree just so.
Strands trickle from his coat. An hour to go.

2

Past Christmas dinners, fused by love, now shine
Like candles on white linen one last time.

Let the wax run until each stick's a growth
Of dark red drippings on the tablecloth.

Reflecting the flames, the glint of cutlery,
Are Christmas bulbs they've saved for years. They'll be

At spring's garage sale. Things will just be things:
Suits, tools, old records, sickroom furnishings.

Simply as for the pepper, one could ask
For gossip, how the new car does on gas,

Though only anger will lay bare the nerve
Where morphine has no purchase, love that hurts:

A flurry of sharp words that turns to snow
Heavily blowing outside their window now,

Which turns the grandkids loose, and the quarrel holds
Just like old times, through pie à la mode,

More coffee. Sugared measurings recur
In which they know there is no future, blur

Like smoky breaths of children playing hard,
One with the other, in the changing yard.

The Condolence

When he lay dying in the hospital
It was as if he couldn't bear my touch,
But he was like that sometimes, afraid of love
Especially when he needed it too much.

I thought I'd sit by him and read, or pray;
Bring up old times that we could smile at now,
Then later, if he wanted, hold his hand
To make it easier for him to go,

Though he still struggled to get out of it,
And stiffened the little that was left of him
Against my comforting, as if he sensed
A darker lullaby than I could hum,

And kept the sliding bed-table between us,
More stubborn as the pain and fear increased.
"Let go, let go," I whispered, desperate
To draw the curtain and get on with grief.

When he grew weak enough I held him close.
We kissed. Then he went mercifully fast.
But that was how it always was with us,
Me needing him, him giving in at last.

Community Hospital

Even the morning is redundant now.
He lays a rosary on the pillowcase
So that the last thing that his father will know
Won't be the Yogi Bear cartoon next door.
The self-importance each fought the other for
At the expense of love comes down to this:
He shaves the not-so-strange, unconscious face
Absurdly, in case there is a visitor;
And from ice water crooks a plastic straw
To the slack mouth, in hopes that he might draw.

Elegy at Donner Hot Springs

Retreating to the hills again, I pump
My lantern brighter, brightest, as I make
Two trees, then farther trees, then river, cliff,
Or turn it down to draw the world in closer,
To make it mine, though the stars wheel.
                                        My hands
Are skilled at turning rocks and killing bait,
Good for wood-gathering and making fire,
For carrying water, a surer use
Than trying to hold on to someone.
                                    Skills
For a small world, one where the lover's feel
For losing and for being lost is lost,
Like hands gone numb in icy river water
When skinning them on stones won't bring back feeling.

I wake up to the honkers' noisy rout
Trimming their ragged V above the dam.
Flaps down, they lean back in their awkward skids,

Breaking the mirror of pretty yellow elms.
It is the anniversary of your death
And I have dreamed you on a ghostly phone.

Deer vanish when I turn my head. At night
I throw log after log on for the geysers
Of orange sparks that seep into the black.
September's first snow prints the reservoir
Dryly, and drives the spawn urge in wild trout,
And the heron too, as if to an old song,
Lifts for the creek dam to await the strongest.

I have my fire, where what I've lost I picture
In shaping flames, in glowing ash at dawn,
Restoring a human face to one disfigured,
Though only love can make one come alive.
But I'm easier with memory that smoothes,
As water smoothes the rocks and mutes the jays,
Than with the raw backtalk of human beings.
I'm easier with loneliness, and find
Myself wading upstream half-naked, shin
Bones aching with the river's glacial past,
Till I come on the hot springs and I sink.

I am all eyes, a tree stump to some birds,
Contented and half-human, currentless
As my emotions dull to ancient grain.
I would almost heal, though I know where that leads,
Somewhere between whitewater and the falls.

Once when I brought my lover here, snow on
Pink manzanita blossoms in the morning

And water grinding down like history
Silenced us in one bag.
Blue lupine, bent in heavy spray, flung drops
Righting itself. And by one falls, scooped rock
Held hundreds of rosy shapes of polished wood.
She chose one with her character, whose grain,
Seeking a pattern that returned itself,
Began perhaps before the portent star;
Nor would she let me steal from time just one
From all my pocketful. What chance had we.

And I remember you, wading the river always,
But cannot make out your face for water's glare,
Each month a feature less, last month the eyes,
This month the mouth and brow as earth in time
And noon sun in my memory do their worst.
That girl I knew for weeks I can remember
Clear as a photo and with all my senses,
But you are only silhouette, a walk
I'll see sometimes in someone. I think you
To life almost, then think of her, whose full
Lips I could think of at your funeral,
The light down of her breasts and her long hair,
Desire destroying grief, and grief desire,
As if I had to choose, as if the way
I felt were up to me, the only way
The smart survivor would consent to feel.

I heal in hot springs where the temperature
Is 110 when the banks pile high with snow,
Time to forget, to melt in waking sleep.
Soon creeks will freeze, blizzards cover the ice,

And then no creeks but furrows in snow meadows.
Nor have I blade of grass, nor lock of hair.
Waters will move beneath thick frozen ice,
But darker, as they move in memory.

Is it sunrise or sunset when the canyon
Reddens, and I come to?
                              I blow the ashes,
Twigs catch, and soon I have my coffee fire,
Still time to fish the last light for my dinner,
To read the river's text attentively,
Each log and riffle, as if there were an author,
To kneel in water with an open hand,
Surprised at last, to let a fine trout go.

At the Family Plot

Amazing, underneath this flowering tree,
(Timothy Dekin 1943–)
The conversation blurring, far off. Me.

King Salmon in the Midwest

Old black mouth, *Oncorhynchus tshawytscha,*
Teach me the dream:
Back to the Chukchi Sea of Alaska and choppy bays,
Each fish deep-bodied, connected:
Great Silvery School
                          reversing itself as one self
Fleeing the killer whale, charging up
The Umpqua and thunderous Columbia,
Silvery voyagers battering themselves to death
Leaping waterfalls,
                          impossibly swimming in air,
Slicing up the last tailrace, into spill gates,
A turbine maelstrom of hydroelectric nights;
Teach me your desire,
Blind, stupid, slavish, suicidal, joyous
Passion for the divine source.

  Your huge dark shadow
                          fanning above the gravel redds,

You are most worthy, too powerful for eagles,
Milt streaming from your anal glands over the clumped roe
Until you wake again as tiny black eyes
In the jellied egg
Or three-inch parr darting through watery sunlight.

But no, no, that is not for you
Hatchery-raised genetic freak of the DNR,
Struggling into the air for one more
Half-leap before death, disoriented,
Laboring the wrong way, or back and forth
Up the Milwaukee River—
I don't know if you know what is happening.
I hope you don't.
In the fish ladder,
                    hoisted convulsing in air,
Squeezed unto death, stripped of yellow
Caviar into plastic buckets,
                          then the empty release
Still fighting upstream.
Teach me to keep going—
Flesh rotting off in chunks while still swimming
In the slow water
Where carcasses make slippery footing underneath,
Gray urban ditch fouled
With dead golf balls and condoms,
Shoulder-to-shoulder snaggers,
                          your dorsal fin and tail
Trailing broken-off lures,
Treble hooks, twenty-pound test line,
The rocks greater than the water
Trickling from drain and sewer pipes now,

And you barely moving,
Food for neighborhood mutts,
Until wedged in a mattress spring you quit at last,
Old Chinook, King Salmon,
Distinctive economic and recreational asset of the State;
Teach me not to pity my lot in life.

Woodmanship

1. Common Snapping Turtle

I almost use as a step
To the riverbank
                  a brown, rounded stone
Big as a manhole cover, inches
From my wader toe.
The three-spiked hind shell reminds me
It's very dangerous to live for only one day at a time
But what other life is there?

At Cedar Lake, when I visited my grandfather
Fifty years ago, lifeguards shot them with .22s
And left them to seethe
With maggots in the mud-skirted cattails.
To wake in whose nightmares but mine!
In my piney-smelling bunk, I woke to rain
On the canvas roof and stole outside

Smelling every lichen.
                              Night was still black in the west
As I hiked ankle-deep in marsh till the sun broke:
One ebony, curved carapace
Steamed in golden light,
Rewarding my seventh summer like the Holy Grail.

I have and have not changed.
                              I gently tap the shell
With the butt of my flyrod for some prehistoric
     adrenaline-inducing,
Lightning-quick snap of the fabled jaws.

But he's hunkered down in Triassic mud,
Triple-ridged tail curled to the side,
Consciousness pulled back from the light,
From my shadow
Filtering through green cypress lace.

I'll wait him out, I decide.
This is my chance to meet my basic mud
Clambering out on thick claws,
The clay made tall,
                         a reunion
Of sorts I can describe
To my young son on the cell phone
From the motel,
                         who can use it for his homework.
Or will *Chelydra serpentina*
Drop his name, back off into atavistic cold depths?
Then there would be no man, motel, telephone, homework.

So on the grassy bank above I sit.
To keep the woods holy
I hunker down with the water's mantra . . .
Ingha dahma, Ingha dahma, Ingha dahma.
Down, down, down, I sink,
Ingha dahma, Ingha dahma, Ingha dahma,
Sinking in effluvial mud,
                              like a lungfish in a drought
Puddle backing into nothingness, closing up . . .

Can I leave things whole,
                              leave the jet-black shell,
Jewel-carved by the morning sun, to maggots?
Is there action borne of awareness alone,
                              like the pure perception
Willingly forgotten,
Like a quick-sprung flower that knows nothing,
Unseeing and unseen
                    deep in the forest?

Suddenly thoughts are on me
                              like no-see-ums on a moose—
In my nose, ears, and nostrils:
A tiny muscle spasm goes off
Like a woodpecker under my armpit . . .
I open my eyes, look down, and find
In rocks
Rearranged beneath my face's reflection
A stranger creature.

2. The Birch Hole

In the still center
Of the stinging black flies,
In the thick
Of the vibrating yellow maggots,
In the singing heart
Of the river,
A jet-black carapace
Pools the continuous river of day and night,
And reflects one lone cypress tree
Rising to the stars.

The mind itself
Becomes the angler's pool.
It reflects his form standing over it,
Casting impotently,
Or gives back only the black unfathomable seal.

Ten thousand times he casts
Into it and comes up empty.
Ten thousand thousand mantras
He repeats over the unruffled velvet
Until he realizes he
Will have to die to everything,
Be completely without desire,
Become invisible,
Like St. Francis, give away
Totally his fears, hopes, pleasures, guilts,

With nothing promised in return,
Whereby the fox and the tortoise
Fear him no more,
And the perfect blue-jay sky turns more blue.

3. Fisherman's Motel

The anglers converse after sundown
With beers or coffee, trading information on flies,
Stream conditions, and fish, in old chairs
On the frayed carpet outside their doors,
While scores of hawk mosquitoes, beetles, and mayflies
Attack the buzzing neon strips in warm night air.
A kid kicks a soccer ball in the drive,
Ignoring calls to bed from the man in room 12,
The unit with the big cooler out front
From which we've seen a large, puffing woman taking
Out dinner. She avoids our eyes.
"Dulcinea's the wife," Henry says proudly,
After introducing himself to our little sportsmen's club.

We're loaded, by the looks of our SUVs:
Our Winston handcrafted bamboo rods
Sticking out, coolers of fancy beer,
Hors d'oeuvres, smoked salmon.
                                        Henry's down
To four black teeth, a twisted arm,
A goofy, ill-worn ball cap, the woman, and the boy,
And that's about it.
Baldwin County Social Services has sent them here
Until whenever. They're homeless, he says,

And with the same enthusiasm in his voice,
He says he himself is mentally handicapped.
But the boy's just fine. As for the wife, well, ha, ha, he's not so sure.

At this point, *A River Runs Through It*
Having turned to *Deliverance,* Dr. Wilson has to tie
Flies in his room, Robert has to call home,
And Jack's got an early wake-up call.

It's down to me and Henry.
In the drive, the boy plays on,
And I'm thinking of my own son and projecting,
Feeling sorry for Henry Jr.,
                          with his options,
The chief of which is his father,
Who isn't the least bit sorry,
But seemingly proud of many things, including his Christianity,
And I'm stuck with hearing all about it,
Too spineless to make my excuses.
                               By the time
The beetles and mosquitoes are stuck to the outdoor lighting,
Henry is onto family values, and how the Wife
And Boy will never be homeless because he,
Henry, is their home whether they're living
Under a bridge or in a junked car.
                              They've had bad luck.
But we should put things behind us, he says.
The Book says Die Daily, burn the work each evening,
And start the new job at the furniture factory at 5 A.M.
Who knows what could happen?
You could make foreman; well, maybe not foreman.

The boy plays on in the drive, oblivious.
I imagine a stream that has been flowing through
Forests and swamps: lonely, wild, solitary, homeless,
Knowing no other bed but a glacier's track,
Expecting only "Lay me down to sleep when we make
The lake," each new morning a Saturday

                              and it's his birthday.
To escape the conversation (I tell myself)
I hear myself saying, "If you want,
I'll take him fishing in the morning
So Dulcinea can sleep in."

4. Cold Flowing River

Early the next morning, I poach
In the Rod and Gun Club, the boy beside me,
In pitch black, making our way by starlight
And the cold flowing river.
We're being careful of sheriffs with sidearms,
I tell him, though an expensive ticket's about
The worst for getting caught these days.

In the preserve of the privileged, I whisper,
Honest men take small breaths to avoid
The smell of wasted, rotting game.
But poachers breathe
                      from the soles of their feet
The blue-ribbon trout streams.
Now pine needles, now pungent, spongy sucking
Give way to commotion: the slapping and thrashing
Of twenty-pound steelhead trout on the shallow gravel—
The bucks are biting each other's tails,

The hens are heavy with roe.
My heart aches.

Then finally there, the long, moon-shimmering slick
Coming down hard into a sucking whirlpool.
In my desire it is already light.

The boy fishes: a crisp, short, roll cast—
And a huge steelie takes the lure deep in the hole.
The trout jerks its massively jawed head once,
Then twice, as if trying to shake off a nightmare.
The boy strikes sideways, downstream,
To set the hook firmly.

I wait, calm, observant, almost indifferent now,
But still the old feeling comes—
Well being. Delight being. Joy being.
The sun breaking,
Birch branch shiny with spilled light
(Is it black on white
                    or white on black?)
The only difference now my knowing enough not to think.

Go Joy. Fly.
I don't need you,
Which is why you've come,
                    welcome back
My childhood's earliest familiar,
Omnipresent
                    except when desired.
Still, if you will,
                    take bread at my hand

Like any unsuspecting creature of the forest,
Eat the trail of crumbs I left
                              to find my way back.

An explosion goes off in the whirlpool:
Silver with a rosy-pink underbelly,
Predatory, unsuspecting, all of creation
Caught in its exquisite contortions,
A steelhead leaps—
The burden of the past and future lifting—
Two feet out of the water
And throws the hook.

I move up beside the boy to praise his effort;
I try to comfort his unfathomable loss.

5. New Friend

In this uncrowded heart are a few names
It beats with. When I was my only one,
I grew wise: I'd be the first not to care.
Telling the four walls to leave me alone.
I only ran away to come back home,
To have them come and get me in the car.

That pro of loneliness on Christmas Eve
In bars, when even the barflies stayed home,
Who held out—who did he think he made pay?
Or was he just the hero of his poem,
A child that holds his breath until he's blue,
Until he passes out and gets his way?

In this uncrowded heart are a few names
It beats with, fear where they won't let him be,
Birth-terror, sudden light, the heart's thud.
Breaking and entering was their specialty.
Already they have made a little fire:
New friend, to older oak, bring your green wood.

Another Day on Earth

Here is my backyard willow tree,
Such a dirty tree
In summer when I was well,
Raining down long jaundiced whips
To snarl the yard and driveway.
But this morning! How wonderful
My tree looks, no longer weeping
Its dandruff and debris into the rain gutters.
The yard-long hanging shoots
Are like blond dreadlocks on a powerful
Sorceress.
        I feel like I could
Get away with anything today.

What about my usual dread of not being capable
Of pushing the loaded shopping cart
From the automatic supermarket doors to my car?
And of the ventilator?

Oh, but there in the fork
Of naked branches is a huge, ugly nest
That summer hid—
Crows or squirrels
Wintering elsewhere—
Or frozen, perhaps;
I did see a dead squirrel by the fence,
Its hazel eyes wide open.

It's just a question of what one chooses
To think about between now and then.

True, the 13-degree January sky
Is somewhat emptied of oxygen
So I can't get my nose close
Enough to chlorophyll, which contains waxy blue-
Black microcrystalline stuff that makes H_2O
In small mosses, liverworts, ferns and manzanita,
Herbaceous and woody plants, bushes, vines, redwoods,
But the names are tasty-
Sounding behind the bones of my face
And the memories, too.
Summer leaves and blossoms,
Why can't we die as beautifully?
                              On a faint breeze
Vanishing.
Or like my mother, on her last day asking,
"Am I dying yet? Really?"
And when I answered yes,
She took a deep, world-including breath
And forgot to exhale.

But look, my five-year-old
Has left his green hooded parka
Hanging from this very chair from which I,
Almost empty of my fears, observe.
In the left-hand pocket are stones,
Lots of stones, sharp-sided, irregular—gravel
Probably from behind his daycare.
Knowing him, he smelled them, put them in his mouth to taste,
Brought them home to hide them
(They make you share everything in daycare)
From Charlie, Melissa, or Bart
And then completely forgot.

It's a question of moving on to the TV cartoons,
Of what you choose to think about.

He'll be home at four
To share his stones with me
When we go out back to pelt that tree.
Aiming at the nest, of course,
Would make him cry
And when he cries, he gets into it,
Gets his feet wet, waters the earth,
Shames the weeping willow,
Then just as completely stops
And a moment later is sparkling
With laughter.
                    A cardinal
Inexplicably appears on a winter's day,
And the next instant
Flies away.

About the Author

Timothy Dekin taught in writing programs at Loyola University, Northwestern University, and Stanford University. He was the recipient of several Illinois Arts Council grants, and his poems have been published in *American Scholar, Southern Review,* and *Three-penny Review.* He was the author of four chapbooks, *Occasional Uncles, Winter Fruit, Carnival,* and *The Errand.* He died in 2001.